Slow Cooker Cookbook

Delicious Slow Cooking Recipes for Super Healthy Slow Cooker Meals

Contents

Introduction

This book contains information on how to cook holiday slow-cooked meals. Like all appliances, the slow cooker has its unique way of doing things. This is why it is important that you understand how it works so you can easily adapt your cooking style accordingly. Yes, slow cookers may be the kind of appliance that allows you to throw the ingredients in and return home to a cooked meal, but you also have to remember that it can't work miracles without your help.

Success in the slow cooker, like success in the oven or just about any kind of kitchen appliance, depends upon using proper cooking techniques.

This cookbook aims to provide you with as many holiday recipes as you can get to incorporate in your list of to-cook food during the holiday season. Plus, all the ingredients are easy to find, so make the most out of your slow cooker during this most wonderful time of the year.

Chapter 1 - Slow Cooker Benefits

Slow cookers are amazingly low maintenance. One usually consists of a metal casing and a stoneware insert with a tight-fitting lid. For easier cleaning and convenience, it is best that you be able to easily remove the insert from the metal casing. The heat source comes from the casing, the electrical coils that surround the stoneware insert. These said coils can be used to power a 100-watt light bulb. And, because the slow cooker only operates with just a small amount of energy, you can leave it turned on without the constant worries of electricity bills rising up to the roof or sudden accidents while you are away from home.

The slow cooker's less-is-better approach is, in many ways, the secret to its success. It does its work by cooking food very slowly – from 200 degrees F on the low setting to 300 degrees F on high. So, what are the benefits of using slow cookers in cooking food? Take note of the following:

- ✓ It enables you to produce delicious pot roasts, soups, briskets, stews, and even desserts. Did you know that you need not worry of not having an oven because with just the use of a slow cooker, you still ensure the success of making even the most delicate of custards and puddings?
- ✓ Once you use this appliance, you would not want to cook your recipes in any other way. You will most definitely prefer having a slow cooker than any other cooking appliance out there.
- ✓ This makes succulent stews that don't stick to the bottom of the pot or dry out.
- ✓ It helps in breaking down even the toughest connective tissue of less tender cuts of meat.
- ✓ It allows seasoning in complex sauces to meld without scorching.
- ✓ It helps you save time because it allows you to forget about the food the moment you put all the ingredients in the slow cooker. However, note that you still have to pay attention to advance preparation in order to ensure slow cooker success. Indeed, it is a great time saver for busy days.

- ✓ It is entertaining worthy. Since the holidays are fast approaching, you will find recipes in this cookbook that are entertaining worthy and definitely a good idea for the great holiday feast.
- ✓ Totally useful all year round. Yes, you can use this any time of the year. Who says you can't have a hot soup during summer days? The perks of using this kind of cooking appliance is that it eliminates the need to use the oven, which makes the already hot summer day even hotter.
- ✓ The beauty in slow cookers is that you can carry one even if you travel. There are easy to carry slow cookers that you can bring along with you when you go on vacation or cook for a family or friend. There are so many models, shapes, and sizes of slow cookers on the market that it is impossible not to stumble upon the one that suits your lifestyle.
- ✓ Slow cookers are energy savers. They are less energy when weighed against the conventional oven.

Chapter 2 – Holiday Soups and Starters

Recipe 1 - Pumpkin Soup

Ingredients:

- 1 tbsp. olive oil
- 1 onion, chopped
- ½ small red onion, cut into wedges
- Fresh root ginger, grated
- 5 cups vegetable stock
- 1 kg pumpkin squash, cut into small chunks
- Pinch of salt
- Pinch of ground pepper
- 4 tbsp. coconut cream
- 1 ripe tomato, chopped
- 1 cup coriander

Directions:

1. Combine olive oil, onion, red onion, root ginger, vegetable stock, pumpkin squash, coriander, tomato, salt, pepper, and coconut cream into the slow cooker. Stir until well-combined.

2. Cover with the lid. Cook on low for 6 hours. Adjust seasoning, if needed. Serve.

Recipe 2 - Beef Bone Broth

Ingredients:

- 4 tbsp. olive oil
- 4 lbs. beef bones with marrow
- 4 garlic cloves, peeled, crushed
- 1 white onion, roughly chopped
- 2 celery stalks, chopped
- 3 carrots, roughly chopped
- 4 tbsp. apple cider vinegar
- 2 fresh bay leaves, whole
- Pinch of sea salt
- Pinch of black pepper
- Water

Directions:

1. Pour half the oil in non-stick skillet. Fry beef bones until brown on all sides. Place beef into the slow cooker.
2. Pour remaining oil and sauté garlic and onion until translucent and fragrant. Add in carrots and celery. Cook until lightly seared. Transfer contents into the slow cooker.
3. Add apple cider vinegar and bay leaves. Pour water until all ingredients are submerged under water.
4. Cover with the lid. Cook bone broth for 6 hours. Turn off heat.
5. Discard solids and strain broth. Season with salt and pepper. Serve.

Recipe 3 - Lamb Bone Broth

Ingredients:

- 4 tbsp. olive oil
- 4 lbs. raw lamb bones with marrow
- 4 garlic cloves, crushed
- 2 white onions, peeled, roughly chopped
- 3 carrots, roughly chopped
- 2 celery stalks, chopped
- 4 tbsp. coconut vinegar
- 2 fresh bay leaves, whole
- 1 handful fresh mint, rinsed, spun-dried
- Water
- Pinch of sea salt
- Pinch of black pepper

Directions:

1. Pour half the oil in non-stick skillet. Fry lamb bones until brown on all sides. Place beef into the slow cooker.
2. Pour remaining oil and sauté garlic and onion until translucent and fragrant. Add in carrots and celery. Cook until lightly seared. Transfer contents into the slow cooker.
3. Pour coconut vinegar and hot water until all ingredients are submerged under water.
4. Cover with the lid. Cook bone broth for 6 hours. Turn off heat. Add mint leaves. Allow to steep for 15 minutes.
5. Discard solids and strain broth. Season with salt and pepper. Serve.

Recipe 4 - Turkey Bone Broth

Ingredients:

- 2 lbs. roasted turkey bones/carcass
- 2 garlic cloves, crushed
- 2 red onions, peeled, chopped
- 2 celery stalks, chopped
- 1 lemon, halved, freshly squeezed, include lemon rinds
- 1 tbsp. whole peppercorns
- 2 dried bay leaves
- 1 pinch fresh rosemary, roughly torn
- 1 pinch fresh thyme, roughly torn
- Water
- Pinch of sea salt
- Pinch of black pepper

Directions:

1. Place turkey bones, garlic, onions, celery, lemon and lemon rinds, whole peppercorns, bay leaves, rosemary, and thyme into the slow cooker.
2. Pour water until all ingredients are submerged under water. Secure lid. Cook on low for 6 hours. Turn off heat. Tip in lemon juice.
3. Discard solids and strain broth. Season with salt and pepper. Serve.

Recipe 5 - Asian-Style Chicken Soup

Ingredients:

- 2 tbsp. olive oil, divided
- 2 lbs. chicken thigh fillets, rinsed
- 4 cups water
- 2 tbsp. fish sauce
- Dash of Spanish paprika
- 2 large unripe papaya, cubed
- ½ cup chili leaves, rinsed
- Pinch of sea salt
- Pinch of black pepper

Aromatics

- 1 thumb-sized ginger, crushed with flat side of knife
- 2 garlic cloves, minced
- 2 onions, minced

Directions:

1. Pour 1 tbsp. of oil into a saucepan. Fry chicken fillets until golden brown. Set aside.
2. Pour remaining oil into pan and sauté ginger, garlic, and onion for 3 minutes or until translucent and fragrant.
3. Transfer everything into the slow cooker. Add fish sauce and paprika. Secure the lid. Cover and cook on low for 4 hours. Add papaya and chili leaves. Reposition the lid and cook on low for another 1 hour.
4. Taste; adjust seasoning if desired. Ladle soup in bowls. Serve.

Recipe 6 - Fresh Asparagus Soup

Ingredients:

- 3 cups vegetable stock
- 3 cups water
- 2 lbs. green asparagus, roughly chopped
- 1 can whole button mushrooms, rinsed, drained
- 1 cup raw cashew nuts, whole
- Pinch of sea salt
- Pinch of black pepper to taste

Garnishes

- ¼ cup sour cream, whisked well
- Pinch fresh parsley, minced

Directions:

1. Pour vegetable stock, water, asparagus, button mushrooms, cashew nits, sea salt, and pepper into a slow cooker.
2. Cover the lid and cook on low for 4 hours or until the cashew nuts are fork tender. Turn off the heat. Adjust seasoning if need.
3. Cool soup before processing in a food processor. Process until smooth. Ladle soup into individual bowls.
4. Drizzle sour cream into soup and sprinkle parsley as garnish. Serve.

Recipe 7 - Ginger Chicken and Mushroom Soup

Ingredients:

- 3 tbsp. olive oil
- 1 lb. portabella mushrooms, caps sliced into thick slivers
- 1 lb. chicken thigh, bone-in
- 3 cups water
- 2 cups chicken bone broth
- Pinch of sea salt
- Pinch of black pepper
- 2 tsp. sesame oil
- 1 zucchini, processed into spaghetti-like noodles
- ¼ cup fresh chives, minced

Aromatics:

- 3 garlic cloves, minced
- 2 white onions, thinly sliced
- 1 thumb-sized ginger, julienned

Directions:

1. Pour 2 tbsp. of olive oil into a saucepan. Fry mushroom slivers for 3 minutes or until seared brown. Set aside.
2. Pour remaining oil and sauté onions until translucent. Add chicken thigh. Pour water and chicken broth. Season with salt and pepper. Transfer all ingredients into the slow cooker. Cover the lid and cook on low for 6 hours.
3. Add zucchini noodles and sesame oil. Reposition the lid and cook on low for 2 hours.
4. Place desired amount of zucchini noodles into soup bowls. Ladle soup on top. Garnish with minced chives. Serve.

Recipe 8 - Cranberry Christmas Soup

Ingredients:

- 4 cups vegetable stock

- 4 cloves garlic, chopped

- 4 beets, coarsely chopped

- Pinch of salt

- Pinch of pepper

- 1 cup cranberries

- 1 orange juice

- 1 orange zest

- 2 tbsp. coconut sugar

- Vegetarian sour cream

- Dill fronds

Directions:

1. Combine stock, garlic, beets, salt, and pepper in a slow cooker. Cover the lid and cook on low for 6 hours.
1. Add cranberries, orange juice, zest, coconut sugar, and beet leaves. Cook on high for another 1 hour.
2. Cool soup lightly and then puree in a blender. Spoon into bowls. Top with sour cream and sprinkle dill.

Recipe 9 - Holiday Milky Broccoli Soup

Ingredients:

- 1 quart vegetable broth

- 2 cups almond milk

- 1 small onion, finely chopped

- 1 package frozen broccoli

- Pinch of black pepper

- 1 cup vegetarian Parmesan cheese

Directions:

1. Mix broth, milk, broccoli, onion, pepper and water in the slow cooker. Cover the lid and cook on high for 3 hours or on low for 6 hours. Turn off the heat.

2. Sprinkle parmesan cheese. Stir until smooth. Serve.

Recipe 10 - Carrot Soup

Ingredients:

- 2 cloves garlic, sliced
- 1 onion, roughly chopped
- 3 carrots, cut into thick pieces
- 2 cups water
- 1 vegetable broth
- 1 can coconut milk
- 1 ground ginger
- 2 tbsp. brown sugar
- Pinch of salt
- Chopped cashews
- Fresh cilantro

Directions:

1. Place garlic and onion over the bottom of the slow cooker. Place carrots on top. Top with carrots. Pour vegetable broth and water.
2. Cover the lid and cook on low for 6 hours or on high for 4 hours.
3. Meanwhile, puree coconut milk, ginger, brown sugar, and salt. Puree until a smooth consistency is achieved.
4. Transfer into soup bowls. Garnish with cashews and cilantro.

Recipe 11 - Odds and Ends Beef and Bean Stew

Ingredients:

- 4 cups beef bone broth
- 1 thumb-sized ginger, crushed
- 2 onions, quartered
- 1 lb. oxtails, trimmed well
- 1 lb. ox tripe, sliced into inch thick squares
- 2 leeks, green parts minced
- 2 lemongrass bulbs, crushed
- 1 tbsp. black peppercorns
- 1 tsp. fish sauce
- 1 lb. snow peas

Directions:

1. Pour bone broth and add ginger, onions, oxtails, ox tripe, leeks, lemongrass, black peppercorns, and fish sauce into the slow cooker. Cover the lid and cook on low for 6 hours or until the oxtail is tender. Turn off heat.
2. Add snow peas. Reposition the lid and cook for another 30 minutes. Allow to rest. Taste; adjust seasoning if needed.
3. Ladle soup into bowls. Serve.

Recipe 12 – Swedish Meatballs

Ingredients:

- 1 lb. lean ground beef
- 1 onion, grated
- 1 egg beaten
- ½ cup almond flour
- 2 tsp. lemon juice, freshly squeezed
- ½ tsp. sea salt
- ½ tsp. freshly ground black pepper
- ½ tsp. all spice
- 2 tbsp. extra virgin olive oil
- 1 tbsp. coconut flour
- ½ tsp. cracked black peppercorns
- 2 cups beef stock
- ½ cup sour cream
- ½ cup dill fonds, chopped

Directions:

1. Combine ground beef, onion, egg, almond flour, lemon juice, zest, salt, pepper, and all spice in a bowl. Mix well. Shape into balls.
2. In a skillet, heat the oil. Cook meatballs in batches for 4 minutes or until browned on all sides. Transfer into the slow cooker. Add coconut flour into the pan and peppercorns. And beef stock. Stir well.
3. Cover the lid and cook on low for 6 hours or on high for 3 hours. Transfer meatballs into a serving dish. Top with sour cream and dill. Serve.

Recipe 13 – Country Terrine

Ingredients:

- 2 lbs. boneless pork shoulder, coarsely chopped
- 4 oz. smoked bacon, cubed
- 8 oz. stewing veal, coarsely chopped
- 1 onion, grated
- 2 garlic cloves, pureed
- 1 tsp. sea salt
- 2 tsp. cracked black peppercorns
- 2 tbsp. cognac
- 2 tbsp. fresh thyme leaves

Directions:

1. In a meat grinder, grind pork, bacon, and veal. Transfer into a bowl. Add onion, garlic, salt, thyme, and cognac. Cover and refrigerate overnight.
2. When ready to cook. Transfer mixture into a pan. Cover tightly with a foil. Secure with a string. Place in the slow cooker and add hot water. Make sure it covers about halfway up the sides of the pan.
3. Cover the lid and cook on low for 8 hours or until a thermometer reads 160F. Chill before serving.

Recipe 14 – Caper Caponata

Ingredients

- 1 tbsp. liquid honey
- 3 tbsp. red wine vinegar
- 2 tsp. extra virgin olive oil
- 1 eggplant, cubed
- 4 garlic cloves, minced
- ¼ cup sun dried tomatoes, finely chopped
- 1 tsp. cracked black peppercorns
- ½ tsp. sea salt
- 2 tbsp. drained capers
- ½ red bell pepper, diced
- ¼ cup parsley leaves, chopped

Directions:

1. Combine honey and vinegar in a bowl. Stir until well combined. Set aside.
2. In a skillet, heat the oil. Add eggplant and cook for 3 minutes, per batch. Add more oil if needed, Transfer into the slow cooker.
3. Add garlic, sun dried tomatoes, salt, and peppercorns.
4. Place a parchment over the eggplant mixture. Cover the lid and cook on low for 6 hours.
5. Lift parchment and discard, taking care not to spill accumulated liquid.
6. Stir in cappers and bell pepper. Cover and cook for another 15 minutes.
7. Transfer into a serving bowl. Garnish with parsley. Serve.

Recipe 15 – Braised Tomato Topping

Ingredients:

- ¼ cup extra virgin olive oil
- 1 can diced tomatoes
- 2 garlic cloves, minced
- 2 tsp. dried oregano
- ½ tsp. sea salt
- 2 tbsp. parsley leaves, finely chopped

Directions:

1. Place 2 tbsp. olive oil into the slow cooker. Swirl to coat. Add garlic, tomatoes, oregano, and salt. Drizzle remaining olive oil. Place a large parchment over tomatoes, pressing it down to brush food and extending up the sides of the slow cooker.
2. Cover the lid and cook on low for 6 hours, Lift parchment out and discard.
3. Stir in parsley. Season with salt and pepper. Transfer to a serving dish. Serve.

Recipe 16 – Maple Orange Pecans

Ingredients:

- ¼ cup pure maple syrup
- ½ tsp. ground cinnamon
- 1 tbsp. orange zest, grated
- Pinch of cayenne pepper
- 2 cups raw pecan, halved

Directions:

1. Mix maple syrup, cinnamon, orange zest, and cayenne pepper in the slow cooker.
2. Cover the lid and cook on high for 1 hour. Add pecans. Stir well.
3. Place a clean towel over the stoneware to absorb moisture. Reposition the lid. Cover and cook on high for another 1 hour or until the nuts are nicely toasted.
4. Spread on a baking sheet. Sprinkle with paprika. Store in an airtight container.

Recipe 17 - Pea and Spinach Soup

Ingredients:

- 2 tbsp. vegetable oil

- 2 tsp. black mustard seeds

- 1 large onion, chopped

- 2 inches ginger, finely grated

- 2 tbsp. curry paste

- ½ tsp. turmeric

- 1 green chili, finely chopped

- 3 ½ cups of water

- 1 ¾ cups coconut milk

- 1 cup frozen peas

- Pinch of salt

- Pinch of ground pepper

- 8 oz. baby leaf spinach

Directions:

1. Heat oil in a pan. Cook mustard seeds for 1 minute or until the seeds pop.

2. Add the onion, ginger, curry paste, turmeric, and chili. Cook for 3 minutes.

3. Pour boiling water into the pan. Put all ingredients into the slow cooker. Pour coconut milk and tip in peas.

4. Cover the lid. Cook on low for 6 hours. Stir in spinach. Reposition the lid. Cook on high for another 10 minutes. Serve.

Recipe 18 - Pumpkin Coconut Soup

Ingredients:

- 2 tbsp. extra virgin olive oil

- 2 onions, finely chopped

- 4 cloves garlic, minced

- 2 stalks celery, diced

- 2 carrots, diced

- 2 tbsp. gingerroot, minced

- 1 tbsp. ground cumin

- Pinch of salt

- Pinch of pepper

- 5 cups vegetable stock

- 6 cups pumpkin, cubed

- ¼ tsp. cayenne pepper

- 2 tbsp. lime juice

- 1 cup coconut milk

Directions:

1. Heat the oil in a pan. Cook onions, garlic, celery, carrots, ginger, cumin, salt, and pepper. Add stock. Bring to a boil. Tip in pumpkin. Transfer into the slow cooker.

2. Cover the lid. Cook on low for 6 hours. Allow to cool before processing a blender.

3. Meanwhile, combine cayenne and lime juice in a bowl. Add into the slow cooker. Pour coconut milk. Reposition the lid. Cook on high for another 15 minutes.

Recipe 19 - Chestnut Sausage

Ingredients:

- 1 tbsp. olive oil

- 5 vegetarian Quorn sausages

- 1 large onion, chopped

- 1 large carrots, cut into chunks

- 1 lb. chestnut mushrooms

- 2 tbsp. plain flour

- 1 tbsp. sage, chopped

- 2 ½ cups vegetable stock

- 1 tbsp. mustard

- 8 oz. pack chestnuts

- 1 courgettes, cut into chunks

- 1 cup cabbage, shredded

- Pinch of salt

- Pinch of pepper

Directions:

1. Heat oil in a pan. Cook sausages for 5 minutes. Add in carrots and mushrooms. Stir well.

2. Sprinkle flour and sage. Pour vegetable stock, mustard, chestnuts, courgettes, cabbage, salt, and pepper. Stir until all ingredients are well coated by flour. Bring to a boil.

3. Put everything into the slow cooker. Cover the lid. Cook on low for 6 hours. Serve.

Chapter 3 – Slow Cooker Meat Mains

Recipe 20 - Chili Beef and Bacon with Blue Cheese Spread

Ingredients:

- 1⅛ cups water, divided
- ½ lb. streaky bacon, diced
- 2½ lbs. ground beef
- 1 onion, minced
- ½ cup kabocha (Japanese pumpkin), diced
- 1 cauliflower head, minced
- 1 fire-roasted diced tomato
- 1 tbsp. smoked paprika
- 1 tbsp. chipotle powder
- ½ tsp. cayenne powder
- 1 tsp. sea salt
- 1 tsp. tomato paste
- ½ tsp. fish sauce
- Pinch of sea salt
- Pinch of black pepper to taste
- ¼ cup blue cheese spread, for garnish
- ⅛ cup fresh chives, minced, for garnish

Directions:

1. Pour 1/8 cup of water into a skillet. Cook the bacon until the water evaporates and bacon starts to crisp. Transfer to a plate. Set aside.
2. Cook ground beef in the same skillet using the bacon grease. Cook until seared and brown on all sides. Remove from heat. Transfer contents into the slow cooker.
3. Place kabocha, cauliflower, tomatoes, smoked paprika, chipotle powder, cayenne powder, sea salt, tomato paste, fish sauce, sea salt, and pepper into the slow cooker. Cover the lid and cook on low for 6 hours.
4. Turn off heat. Stir in blue cheese spread. Adjust taste as needed.
5. Ladle into bowls. Garnish with bacon bits and chives. Serve.

Recipe 21 – Slow-Cooked Lemon-Garlic Chicken

Ingredients:

- 4 garlic heads, leave bulb intact
- 2½ pounds chicken, separate chicken breast skin from meat without removing it
- 2 tbsp. each parsley and lemon butter
- 1 tbsp. Spanish paprika powder
- 1 lemon, zested, freshly squeezed
- 1 tbsp. sea salt
- 1 tsp. black pepper
- ¼ cup balsamic vinegar
- ¼ cup water
- Olive oil

Directions:

1. Place whole garlic heads into the slow cooker forming a square. Rub parsley and lemon butter in between chicken skin and breast. Put lemon rinds inside the chicken cavity.
2. Meanwhile, combine paprika powder, lemon zest, salt, and pepper in a bowl. Mix well. Rub mixture into the chicken. Truss chicken and tuck tightly against its sides.
3. Sit chicken on top of the garlic heads. Pour balsamic vinegar, water, and lemon juice. Drizzle in olive oil and sprinkle salt to taste.
4. Cover the lid and cook on low for 6 hours. Turn off heat. Discard lemon rinds and garlic. Serve.

Recipe 22 - Pork Leg with Tatsoi

Ingredients:

- 2½ pounds pork leg, trimmed well
- 1 lb. tatsoi, ends trimmed
- 1 tbsp. balsamic vinegar
- 1 tsp. garlic powder, optional
- ¼ cup coconut oil
- Pinch of sea salt
- Water

Directions:

1. Rub sea salt over pork leg. Transfer into the slow cooker and place in the middle.
2. Pour just enough water until halfway up the meat. Cover the lid. Cook on low for 8 hours or until the pork is fork-tender.
3. Stir in balsamic vinegar, coconut oil, and tatsoi. Reposition the lid and cook for another 1 hour. Turn off heat. Taste; adjust seasoning if needed.
4. Transfer to a plate. Set aside 10 minutes before carving. Serve.

Recipe 23 - Savory Cocoa-Flavored Baby Back Ribs

Ingredients:

- 3 lbs. pork baby back ribs

Dry rub

- 2 tbsp. sea salt
- 2 tbsp. onion powder
- 1 tbsp. garlic powder
- 1 tbsp. ginger powder
- 1 tbsp. cayenne powder
- 2 tbsp. smoky paprika powder
- 1 tbsp. cinnamon powder
- 1 tbsp. oregano powder
- 1 tbsp. mustard powder
- ½ cup unsweetened cocoa powder
- ½ tbsp. white pepper
- ¼ tbsp. red pepper flakes

Directions:

1. Combine sea salt, onion powder, garlic powder, ginger powder, cayenne powder, smoky paprika powder, cinnamon powder, oregano powder, mustard powder, cocoa powder, white pepper, and red pepper flakes in a bowl. Mix well. Rub generously all over baby back ribs.
2. Place ribs inside the slow cooker. Cover the lid and cook on low for 8 hours. Slice ribs between bones. Serve.

Recipe 24 - Spicy Pork and Beef Cheese Chili

Ingredients:

- 2 tbsp. olive oil
- ½ pound streaky bacon, diced
- 1 onion, minced
- 2 garlic cloves, minced
- 1 lb. ground beef
- 1 lb. ground pork
- 1 can peeled and diced tomatoes
- 1 cup beef bone broth
- 2 tbsp. chili powder
- 1 tbsp. cayenne powder
- 1 tbsp. dried oregano, crumbled
- 2 fresh jalapeño peppers, minced
- 1 fresh bird's eye chili, minced
- Dash of red pepper flakes
- ⅛ tbsp. black pepper
- 8 oz. natural cheddar cheese curd
- Pinch of sea salt, only if needed

Directions:

1. Pour oil into a nonstick skillet. Cook bacon until crisp. Sauté garlic and onion for 3 minutes or until translucent and fragrant. Stir in ground pork and beef. Cook until brown all over. Transfer into the slow cooker.
2. Stir in tomatoes, beef broth, chili powder, cayenne powder, dried oregano, jalapeño pepper, bird's eye chili, red pepper flakes, and black pepper. Cover the lid and cook on low for 6 hours.
3. Turn off heat. Add cheese curds. Season with salt. Ladle into bowls. Cool slightly before serving.

Recipe 25 - Veal Roast with Mushroom Sauce

Ingredients:

- 3 tbsp. olive oil, divided
- 2½ lbs. veal shoulder, bone-in
- 1 lb. fresh porcini mushrooms, sliced into ¼-inch pieces
- ¾ cup water
- 2 cups beef bone broth
- 3 tbsp. balsamic vinegar
- 1 leek, minced
- ¼ cup red bell pepper, julienned
- Pinch of sea salt
- Pinch of black pepper to taste

Directions:

1. Pour half of the olive oil into the skillet. Cook veal shoulders until brown on all sides. Set aside. Tip in mushrooms and cook until lightly brown on both sides. Transfer into the slow cooker.
2. Pour water, bone broth, balsamic vinegar, leek, red bell pepper, salt, and pepper into the slow cooker. Cover the lid and cook on low for 6 hours.
3. Turn off heat. Transfer meat for carving. Allow to sit for 10 minutes before thinly slicing. Arrange on a platter. Serve.

Recipe 26 – Holiday Pork with Tomatoes and White Beans

Ingredients:

- 2 tsp. olive oil
- ¾ lb. pork tenderloin, fat trimmed, sliced into half-inch round
- ¼ cup shallots, finely chopped
- 14 ½ ounces tomatoes, fire-roasted, crushed
- ½ cup chicken broth
- 3 cups spinach
- 15 oz. cannellini white kidney beans
- 2 tbsp. balsamic vinegar

Directions:

1. Heat oil in a skillet. Cook tenderloin slices for 4 minutes on each side. Transfer into the slow cooker.
2. Stir in shallots, tomatoes, chicken broth, spinach, beans, and balsamic vinegar into the slow cooker. Cover the lid and cook on low for 6 hours.
3. Turn off heat. Adjust taste, if needed. Serve.

Recipe 27 - Balsamic Pork

Ingredients:

- 2 tsp. olive oil
- 4 pork loin chops, five-ounce, boneless, w/ fat trimmed
- ½ tsp. salt
- 1/3 cup vinegar, balsamic
- 3 twists black pepper, freshly ground
- 1 garlic clove, minced
- ½ cup chicken broth, low-sodium, fat-free

Directions:

1. Pour oil into the skillet. Cook pork loin chops for 4 minutes or until lightly brown on all sides. Transfer into the slow cooker.
2. In the same skillet, sauté garlic for 2 minutes or until fragrant. Transfer into the slow cooker.
3. Pour balsamic vinegar and chicken broth. Cover the lid and cook on low for 4 hours.
4. Turn off heat. Adjust taste, if needed. Serve.

Recipe 28 – Braised Brisket with Gravy

Ingredients:

- 2 tbsp. clarified butter
- 4 lbs. double beef brisket, trimmed
- 2 onions, thinly sliced
- 5 garlic cloves, minced
- 4 celery stalks, diced
- 1 tbsp. ground cumin
- 2 tsp. dried oregano
- 1 cinnamon stick
- 1 tsp. cracked black peppercorns
- ½ tsp. sea salt
- 1 can tomatoes with juice
- 1 cup chicken stock
- 2 cups boiling water
- 3 dried guajillo chiles
- 1 jalapeño pepper, diced
- 1 cup cilantro
- 1 green bell pepper, diced

Directions:

1. Heat oil in a skillet. Add brisket and cook for 6 minutes or until brown on all sides. Transfer into the slow cooker.
2. Add remaining butter. Cook onions, garlic, celery, cumin, oregano, cinnamon stick, peppercorns, and sea salt. Stir well. Add tomatoes with juice, stock, and water. Bring to a boil.
3. Transfer all ingredients in to the slow cooker. Cover the lid and cook on low for 8 hours.
4. Soak chiles. Cook for another 30 minutes. Discard stems and soaking liquid.
5. Transfer mixture into a blender. Add jalapeño and cilantro. Puree and add into the slow cooker. Add bell pepper.

6. Reposition the lid and cook on high for 20 minutes. Serve.

Recipe 29 – Wine-Braised Oxtails with Mushrooms

Ingredients:

- 2 tbsp. clarified butter
- 4 lbs. oxtails, cut into 2-inch pieces
- 2 onions, finely chopped
- 3 garlic cloves, minced
- 2 celery stalks, diced
- 2 carrots, diced
- 1 tsp. dried thyme leaves
- ½ tsp. sea salt
- ½ cracked black peppercorns
- 1 bay leaf
- 1 ½ cups dry red wine
- 1 can tomatoes with juice
- 12 oz. mushrooms, quartered
- ½ cup parsley leaves, finely chopped

Directions:

1. Heat 1 tbsp. of butter in a skillet. Cook oxtails, in batches, and cook for 4 minutes or until lightly browned all over. Transfer into the slow cooker.
2. Add remaining butter. Cook onions, garlic, celery, carrots, thyme, sea, salt, peppercorns, and bay leaf. Stir well.
3. Pour wine and bring to a boil. Scrape brown bits from bottom of the pan. Add tomatoes with juice.
4. Transfer all ingredients into the slow cooker. Add mushrooms. Cover the lid and cook on low for 8 hours. Discard bay leaves. Garnish with parsley.

Recipe 30 – Holiday Pot Roast

Ingredients:

- 2 tbsp. clarified butter
- 2 oz. pancetta, diced
- 2 onions, finely chopped
- 4 garlic cloves, minced
- 2 celery stalks, diced
- 2 carrots, diced
- 1 tsp. dried rosemary leaves
- 2 bay leaves
- 1 cinnamon stick
- ½ tsp. sea salt
- ½ tsp. cracked black peppercorns
- 2 tbsp. tomato paste
- 3 cups red wine
- Pinch of sea salt
- Pinch of ground black pepper

Directions:

1. Heat 1 tbsp. clarified butter in a skillet. Cook pancetta for 3 minutes on each side until browned. Transfer into the slow cooker.
2. Add beef and cook for 8 minutes or until brown on all sides. Transfer into the slow cooker.
3. In the same skillet, add remaining clarified butter. Sauté onion, garlic, celery, carrots, rosemary, bay leaves, cinnamon stick, sea salt, and peppercorns. Stir in tomato paste. Pour wine. Stir well. Bring to a boil.
4. Transfer into the slow cooker. Cover the lid and cook on low for 8 hours.
5. Transfer meat to a platter. Keep warm. Discard bay leaves. Puree sauce using an immersion blender. Adjust taste if needed. Slice meat and serve.

Recipe 31 – Holiday-Style Oxtails with Celery

Ingredients:

- 2 tbsp. olive oil, divided
- 4 oz. pancetta, diced
- 4 lbs. oxtails cut into 2-inch pieces
- 1 onion, diced
- 2 garlic cloves, minced
- 2 celery stalks, diced
- 1 tsp. sea salt
- 1 tsp. black peppercorns
- 1 cup dry white wine
- 1 cup tomato paste
- 2 cups chicken stock
- 6 cups celery, sliced
- ½ cup parsley loves, finely chopped

Directions:

1. Heat olive oil in a skillet Add pancetta and cook for 4 minutes until browned on all sides. Transfer into the slow cooker.
2. Add oxtails, and cook in batches, for 5 minutes or until brown on all sides. Transfer into the slow cooker.
3. Heat the remaining oil. Sauté onion, garlic, celery, sea salt, and peppercorns for 4 minutes. Pour wine. Scrape up brown bits. Stir in tomato paste and chicken stock.
4. Transfer into the slow cooker. Cover the lid and cook on low for 8 hours.
5. When oxtails are almost cooked, bring a pot with salted water to a boil. Add celery and oxtails. Transfer into the slow cooker again. Cover and cook on high for 10 minutes. Garnish with parsley. Serve.

Recipe 32 – Christmas Beef with Horseradish Cream

Ingredients:

- 2 tbsp. olive oil
- 2 lbs. stewing beef, trimmed
- 2 onions, finely chopped
- 3 garlic cloves, minced
- 2 celery stalks, diced
- 1 bay leaf
- ½ tsp. sea salt
- ½ tsp. cracked black peppercorns
- 4 whole cloves
- 8 whole allspice
- 1 cup dry red wine
- 1 tbsp. red wine vinegar
- 3 cups beef stock
- 1 tbsp. coconut sugar
- 4 medium beets, cubed
- 2 tbsp. homemade horseradish
- 1/2 cup crème fraiche

Directions:

1. In a skillet, heat the oil set over medium-high heat. Cook beef, in batches, for 5 minutes or until lightly browned. Transfer into the slow cooker.
2. Heat the remaining oil. Sauté onion, garlic, celery, bay leaf, sea salt, and peppercorns for 3 minutes. Tie cloves and allspice in a cheesecloth. Add to the pan. Pour wine, vinegar, stock, and coconut sugar. Bring to a boil.
3. Transfer everything into the slow cooker. Stir in beets. Cover the lid and cook on low for 8 hours. Discard bay leaf, cloves, and allspice.
4. Meanwhile, in a bowl, combine horseradish and crème fraiche. Stir well. Serve with beef.

Recipe 33 – Italian- Style Goulash

Ingredients:

- 2 tbsp. olive oil
- 2 lbs. stewing beef, trimmed
- 2 onions, diced
- 2 garlic cloves, minced
- 2 celery stalks, diced
- 1 carrot, diced
- 2 tsp. dried oregano
- 1 tsp. dried rosemary
- ½ tsp. sea salt
- ½ tsp. cracked black peppercorns
- ¼ cup tomato paste
- 1 cup dry red wine
- 2 potatoes, diced
- 2 cups beef stock
- 1 tsp. hot paprika
- 1 tbsp. sweet paprika
- 2 tbsp. water

Directions:

1. Heat oil in a skillet. Cook beef, in batches, for 5 minutes or until lightly browned. Transfer into the slow cooker.
2. Heat the remaining oil. Sauté onion, garlic, celery, carrot, oregano, rosemary, sea salt, and peppercorns for 7 minutes. Stir in tomato paste. Pour wine. Bring to a boil. Scrape up brown bits from the bottom of the pan. Transfer into the slow cooker.
3. Add potatoes and pour stock. Cover the lid and cook on low for 8 hours.
4. Meanwhile, in a bowl, dissolve hot and sweet paprika in water. Stir well. Add to the slow cooker. Reposition the lid. Cover and cook on high for 15 minutes. Serve.

Recipe 34– Ranch House Holiday Chicken

Ingredients:

- 1 tbsp. olive oil
- 2 lbs. ground steak, patted dry
- 2 onions, thinly sliced
- 3 garlic cloves, minced
- 3 celery stalks, thinly sliced
- ½ tsp. sea salt
- 1 tsp. cracked black peppercorns
- 1 cup chicken stock
- ¼ tsp. cayenne pepper
- 1 tsp. sweet paprika
- ¼ cup sour cream
- 2 jalapeño peppers

Directions:

1. Heat olive oil in a skillet set over medium-high heat. Cook steak in pieces for 5 minutes or until brown on all sides. Transfer into the slow cooker.
5. Reduce heat. Sauté onion, garlic, celery, sea salt, and peppercorns for 5 minutes. Stir in tomato paste. Pour stock. Bring to a boil. Scrape up brown bits from the bottom of the pan. Transfer into the slow cooker.
2. Cover the lid. Cook on low for 8 hours or on high for 4 hours.
3. Meanwhile, in a bowl, combine cayenne pepper, paprika, and sour cream. Mix until well blended. Add into the slow cooker. Add jalapeno pepper.
4. Reposition the lid. Cook on high for 15 minutes. Serve.

Recipe 35 – Holiday Bolognese Sauce

Ingredients:

- 1 cup hot water
- 1 package dried porcini mushrooms
- 1 tbsp. olive oil
- 2 oz. chunk pancetta, diced
- 1 lb. lean ground beef
- 8 oz. ground pork
- 2 onions, diced
- 4 garlic cloves, minced
- 2 carrots, diced
- 2 celery stalks, diced
- 2 bay leaves
- 1 tbsp. dried Italian seasoning
- ½ tsp. ground cinnamon
- ½ tsp. sea salt
- ½ tsp. cracked black peppercorns
- 1 cup dry red wine
- ¼ cup tomato paste
- 1 can tomatoes with juice, coarsely chopped

Directions:

1. In a bowl, pour hot water. Soak dried mushrooms. Allow to stand for 30 minutes. Drain and reserve liquid. Pat mushrooms dry and finely chop/ Set aside.
2. Meanwhile, heat the oil in a skillet. Cook pancetta for 5 minutes or until browned. Transfer into the slow cooker.
3. In the same skillet, add oil. Cook beef and pork. Add onions, garlic, carts, celery, bay leaves, Italian seasoning, cinnamon, mushrooms, salt, and pepper.
4. Pour wine. Bring to a boil. Scrape up brown bits from the bottom of the pan. Add mushroom liquid.

5. Transfer into the slow cooker. Add tomato paste and tomatoes with juice. Cover the lid and cook on low for 8 hours. Serve.

Recipe 36 – Christmas Pork Roast with Rum

Ingredients:

- 3 lbs. boneless pork shoulder, trimmed
- 1 piece gingerroot, cut into thin slivers
- 5 garlic cloves, cut into thin slivers
- 1 tsp. dry mustard
- 2 tbsp. coconut sugar
- 1 lime juice, zested, freshly squeezed
- ½ dry rum
- 1 tsp. sea salt
- 1 tsp. cracked black peppercorns
- ½ chili pepper, minced
- 1 tbsp. arrowroot, dissolved in 2 tbsp. cold water

Directions:

1. Make small slits on all sides of the meat, insert ginger and garlic slivers. Pat roast dry with paper towel.
2. Meanwhile, in a bowl, combine mustard and coconut sugar. Rub mixture all over the meat. Place under broiler. Broil for 15 minutes, making sure all sides are browned. Transfer into the slow cooker.
3. In another bowl. Combine lime juice and zest, rum, salt, and peppercorns. Put pork roast. Cover the lid. Cook on low for 8 hours.
4. Remove from the slow cooker and allow to warm. Add chili pepper and arrowroot mixture. Serve with the pork.

Recipe 37 – Braised Lamb Shanks

Ingredients:

- 2 tbsp. olive oil
- 4 large lamb shanks, patted dry
- 3 onions, finely chopped
- 6 garlic cloves, minced
- 2 stalks celery, diced
- 2 carrots, diced
- 1 tsp. dried thyme
- 1 tsp. sea salt
- 1 tsp. cracked black peppercorns
- 1 can tomatoes with juice
- 1 cup dry white wine
- 1 cup chicken stock

For the Lemon Gremolata

- 2 garlic cloves, minced
- 1 cup parsley leaves, finely chopped
- 1 tbsp. extra-virgin olive oil

Directions:

1. In a skillet, heat the oil. Add lamb, in batches, and cook for 8 minutes until brown on all sides. Transfer into the slow cooker.
2. Add remaining oil, sauté onion, garlic, celery, carrots, thyme, sea salt, and peppercorns for 4 minutes. Pour wine. Bring to a boil. Scrape up brown bits from the bottom of the pan. Add mushroom liquid.
3. Transfer into the slow cooker. Add tomatoes with juice and chicken. Cover the lid and cook on low for 6 hours.
4. To make the lemon gremolata, combine olive oil, lemon zest, parsley, and garlic. Mix well. Serve with meat.

Recipe 38 – Christmas Ratatouille

Ingredients:

- 2 tbsp. extra virgin olive oil
- 2 medium eggplants, cubed
- 2 onions, finely chopped
- 4 garlic cloves, minced
- 1 tsp. dried oregano
- ½ tsp. sea salt
- ½ tsp. cracked black peppercorns
- 2 tbsp. red wine vinegar
- 1 can tomatoes with juice, coarsely chopped
- 1 green bell pepper
- 1 lb. okra, cut into 1-inch lengths

Directions:

1. Heat olive oil in a skillet. Cook eggplant, in batches, for 5 minutes or until browned on all sides. Transfer into the slow cooker.
2. Sauté onions, garlic, oregano, sea salt, and peppercorns for 2 minutes. Add in red wine vinegar and tomatoes with juice. Bring to a boil. Transfer into the slow cooker.
3. Cover the lid. Cook on low for 6 hours. Add bell pepper and okra. Reposition the lid. Cover and cook on high for 30 minutes. Serve.

Recipe 39 - Veggie Chili with Cornbread

Ingredients:

- 1 tbsp. olive oil

- 1 large onion, cut into wedges

- 2 garlic cloves, crushed

- 1 red bell peppers, cut into chunks

- 1 large zucchini, cut into chunks

- 2 tsp. chili powder

- 2 tbsp. plain flour

- 1 ½ cups vegetable stock

- 2 tbsp. tomato puree

- 14 oz. canned tomatoes, chopped

- Pinch of salt

- Pinch of pepper

- 1 cup sweetcorn

- 14 oz. canned red kidney

Directions:

1. Heat oil in a pan. Sauté onion, garlic, bell peppers, zucchini, and chili powder for 4 minutes. Stir in flour.

2. Pour vegetable stock, tomato puree, and chopped tomatoes. Bring to a boil. Transfer everything into the slow cooker. Cover the lid. Cook on low for 4 hours.

3. Stir in sweetcorn and kidney beans. Season with salt and pepper. Let it simmer for 10 minutes. Serve.

Recipe 40 - Vegan Risotto with Peas

Ingredients:

- 2 tbsp. olive oil

- 2 fennel bulbs, finely chopped

- 2 garlic cloves, crushed

- lemon rind, finely grated

- lemon juice

- 5 cups vegetable stock

- 1 ½ cup vegan risotto rice

- 1 cup frozen peas

- Pinch of salt

- Pinch of pepper

- Parmesan cheese

Directions:

1. Heat oil in a pan. Sauté fennel bulbs and garlic. Tip in rind and juice. Stir occasionally for 5 minutes or until the fennel begins soften.

2. Pour vegetable stock and rice. Bring to a boil. Transfer everything into the slow cooker. Cover the lid. Cook on low for 4 hours.

3. Stir in peas. Season with salt and pepper. Serve with Parmesan cheese.

Recipe 41 - Moroccan Vegetable

Ingredients:

- 2 tbsp. olive oil

- 1 large onion, cut into thin wedges

- 2 tsp. garlic, minced

- 2 carrots, diced

- 1 lb. butternut squash, cut into small chunks

- 2 tsp. ginger, minced

- 1 tsp. ground turmeric

- 1 large courgette

- 14 0z canned tomatoes, chopped

- 1 tbsp. harissa paste

- 1 large red bell pepper, diced

- 1 ¼ cups vegetable stock

- Pinch of salt

- Pinch of pepper

- 4 ½ oz. baby spinach

- 14 oz. canned chickpeas

- 2 tbsp. maple syrup

- Handful of fresh mint

- Handful of coriander

- Brown rice

Directions:

1. Heat oil in a pan. Sauté onion, garlic, carrots, and butternut squash for 5 minutes or until vegetables are tender. Tip in

2. Stir in ginger, turmeric, courgettes, tomatoes, harissa, bell pepper, and vegetable stock. Season with salt and pepper. Bring mixture to a boil. Transfer into the slow cooker. Cover the lid. Cook on low for 8 hours.

3. Stir in spinach, chickpeas, maple syrup, mint, and half the coriander. Serve on top of brown rice.

Chapter 4 – Holiday Desserts and Snacks

Recipe 42 – Christmas Apples

Ingredients:

- 1 cup dried cranberries
- ½ cup toasted walnuts
- 2 tbsp. coconut sugar
- 1 tsp. orange zest, grated
- 7 apples, cored
- 1 cup pomegranate juice

Directions:

1. Combine cranberries, walnuts, coconut sugar, and orange zest in a bowl. Stuff the apples with the mixture. To do this, hold the apple over the bottom and use your fingers in packing mixture into the core space.
2. Place apples into the slow cooker, Drizzle pomegranate juice.
3. Cover the lid. Cook on low for 6 hours. Transfer apples to a serving dish. Spoon juices. Serve.

Recipe 43 – Apple Cider Compote

Ingredients:

- 3 cups apple cider
- ½ cup coconut sugar
- 2 slices gingerroot, peeled
- 7 firm apples, cored
- Coconut whipped cream

Directions:

1. Combine apple cider, coconut sugar, and gingerroot in a slow cooker. Add apples. Stir well.
2. Cover the lid, cook on high for 2 hours. Transfer into a serving dish. Chill before serving.
3. To serve, ladle into a bowls. Top with coconut whipped cream.

Recipe 44 - Apple, Banana and Chia Seed Parfait

Ingredients:

- 1 tbsp. cashew nuts, chopped, fresh toasted on dry pan, for garnish, optional

Parfait base

- 2 tbsp. chia seeds
- 1 large overripe banana, mashed
- 1¼ cups almond milk, chilled well
- ½ tsp. cinnamon powder
- ⅛ tsp. nutmeg powder

Apple jam

- 2 large Fuji apples, cored, diced
- 2 tbsp. chia seeds
- ¾ cup 100% organic apple juice, unsweetened
- ¾ tsp. cinnamon powder
- ⅛ tsp. nutmeg powder
- Pinch of sea salt

Directions:

1. Mix parfait base ingredients in a bowl. Chill in fridge until ready to assemble.
2. Place apple jam ingredients in the slow cooker. Cover the lid. Cook on low for 4 hours. Turn off heat. Using a potato masher, mash half of jam. Set aside to cool completely to room temperature.
3. To assemble: alternately spoon 2 tbsp. of both parfait base and apple jam into 2 tall parfait glasses until filled almost to the top (or until separate components run out.) Garnish with cashew nuts if using; serve.

Recipe 45 - Ginger Apricot Jam

Ingredients:

- ¼ cup water
- 1 cup raw organic honey
- ½ lemon, fresh juiced, pips removed
- 2 lbs. apricots, unpeeled, pitted, diced
- 1 thumb-sized fresh ginger, peeled, crushed with flat side of knife
- Pinch of sea salt

Directions:

1. Pour water, honey, lemon juice, apricots, ginger, and sea salt in the slow cooker. Cover the lid. Cook on low for 4 hours.
2. Roughly mash some (not all) fruits using a wooden spoon; cook until most of liquid has evaporated, stirring frequently. Turn off heat. Fish out and discard ginger. Cool completely to room temperature before storing in airtight container; use as needed.

Recipe 46 - Ginger Salmonberry Jam

Ingredients:

- 2½ lbs. fresh salmonberries, rinsed, drained
- 2 tsp. ginger powder
- 1 cup raw organic honey
- ¼ cup water
- ½ lemon, fresh juiced, pips removed
- Pinch of sea salt

Directions:

1. Place salmonberries, ginger powder, organic honey, water, lemon juice, and salt in a slow cooker. Cover the lid. Cook on low for 4 hours.
2. Roughly mash fruits using a wooden spoon; cook until most of liquid has evaporated, stirring frequently. Turn off heat. Cool to room temperature before storing in airtight container; use as needed.

Recipe 47 - Mixed Stone Fruit Jam

Ingredients:

- ¼ cup water
- 1 cup raw organic honey
- 1 tsp. cinnamon powder
- ½ pound nectarines, unpeeled, pitted, diced
- ½ pound apricots, unpeeled, pitted, diced
- ½ pound plums, unpeeled, pitted, diced
- ½ pound peaches, unpeeled, pitted, diced
- ½ large lemon, fresh juiced, pips removed
- Pinch of sea salt

Directions:

1. Place water, organic honey, cinnamon powder, nectarines, apricots, plums, peaches, lemon juice, and salt in a slow cooker. Cover the lid. Cook on low for 4 hours.
2. Roughly mash fruits using a wooden spoon; cook until most of liquid has evaporated, stirring frequently. Turn off heat. Cool to room temperature before storing in airtight container; use as needed.

Recipe 48 - Pepper-Apricot Jam

Ingredients:

- 2 lbs. apricots, unpeeled, pitted, diced
- 1 cup raw organic honey
- ¼ cup water
- 1 large fresh Thai green chili, deseeded, minced
- ½ large lemon, fresh juiced, pips removed
- Pinch of sea salt

Directions:

1. Place apricots, honey, water, Thai green chili, lemon juice, and sea salt in a slow cooker. Cover the lid. Cook on low for 4 hours.
2. Roughly mash fruits and peppers using a wooden spoon; cook until most of liquid has evaporated, stirring frequently. Turn off heat. Cool completely to room temperature before storing in airtight container with tight fitting lid; use as needed.

Recipe 49 - Peppery Berry Jam

Ingredients:

- 1 cup frozen boysenberries, thawed
- 1 cup frozen cranberries, thawed
- 1 cup frozen raspberries, thawed
- 1 cup raw organic honey
- ¼ cup water
- 1 large jalapeño pepper, deseeded, minced
- ½ large lemon, fresh juiced, pips removed
- Pinch of sea salt

Directions:

1. Place boysenberries, cranberries, raspberries, honey, water, jalapeno pepper, lemon, and sea salt in a slow cooker. Cover the lid. Cook on low for 4 hours.
2. Roughly mash fruits and peppers using a wooden spoon; cook until most of liquid has evaporated, stirring frequently. Turn off heat. Cool completely to room temperature before storing in airtight container with tight fitting lid; use as needed.

Recipe 50 - Peppery Berry and Currant Jam

Ingredients:

- 1½ cups frozen black or red currants, thawed
- 1½ cups frozen cloudberries, thawed
- 1 cup raw organic honey
- ¼ cup water
- 1 large habañero pepper, deseeded, minced
- 1 large jalapeño pepper, deseeded, minced
- ½ large lemon, fresh juiced, pips removed
- Pinch of sea salt

Directions:

1. Place currants, cloudberries, honey, water, habanero pepper, jalapeño pepper, lemon juice, and sea salt in a slow cooker. Cover the lid. Cook on low for 4 hours.
2. Roughly mash fruits and peppers using a wooden spoon; cook until most of liquid has evaporated, stirring frequently. Turn off heat. Cool completely to room temperature before storing in airtight container with tight fitting lid; use as need.

Recipe 51 - Peppery Pineapple Jam

Ingredients:

- 3 large lime, fresh squeezed, pips removed
- 2 red bird's eye chili, deseeded, minced
- 2 green banana chili, deseeded, minced
- 1 fresh, slightly overripe pineapple, peeled, eyes removed, cored, pulp diced
- 1 cup raw organic honey
- ¼ cup water
- 1 tsp. cinnamon powder
- Pinch of sea salt

Directions:

1. Place lime, bird's eye chili, banana chili, pineapple, honey, water, cinnamon powder, and sea salt in a slow cooker. Cover the lid. Cook on low for 4 hours.
2. Roughly mash fruits and peppers using a wooden spoon; cook until most of liquid has evaporated, stirring frequently. Turn off heat. Cool completely to room temperature before storing in airtight container with tight fitting lid; use as needed.

Recipe 52 - Peppery Red Berry Jam

Ingredients:

- 1 cup frozen cranberries, thawed
- 1 cup frozen raspberries, thawed
- 1 cup raw organic honey
- ¼ cup water
- 1 lb. frozen strawberries, thawed, quartered
- 1 bird's eye chili, deseeded, minced
- 1 ghost chili pepper, deseeded, minced
- 1 Serrano pepper, deseeded, minced
- ½ lemon, fresh juiced, pips removed
- Pinch of sea salt

Directions:

1. Place apricots, honey, water, Thai green chili, lemon juice, and sea salt in a slow cooker. Cover the lid. Cook on low for 4 hours.
2. Roughly mash fruits and peppers using a wooden spoon; cook until most of liquid has evaporated, stirring frequently. Turn off heat. Cool completely to room temperature before storing in airtight container with tight fitting lid; use as needed.

Recipe 53 - Raspberry Jam with Chia Seeds

Ingredients:

- 3 cups fresh raspberries
- 1 cup raw organic honey
- ¼ cup water
- 2 tbsp. chia seeds
- 1 tbsp. lemon juice, fresh squeezed

Directions:

1. Place raspberries, honey, water, chia seeds, and lemon in a slow cooker. Cover the lid. Cook on low for 4 hours.
2. Roughly mash fruits and peppers using a wooden spoon; cook until most of liquid has evaporated, stirring frequently. Turn off heat. Cool completely to room temperature before storing in airtight container with tight fitting lid; use as needed.

Recipe 54 - Strawberry Jam with Flax Seeds

Ingredients:

- 2 tbsp. flaxseeds
- 1 tbsp. lemon juice, fresh squeezed
- 1 lb. frozen strawberries, thawed, drained
- 1 cup raw organic honey
- ¼ cup water

Directions:

1. Place flaxseeds, lemon juice, strawberries, honey, and water in a slow cooker. Cover the lid. Cook on low for 4 hours.
2. Roughly mash fruits and peppers using a wooden spoon; cook until most of liquid has evaporated, stirring frequently. Turn off heat. Cool completely to room temperature before storing in airtight container with tight fitting lid; use as needed.

Recipe 55 - Summer Berry Jam

Ingredients:

- 1 small lemon, fresh juiced, pips removed
- 2 cups frozen blackberries, thawed
- 2 cups frozen black currants, thawed
- 1 cup frozen raspberries, thawed
- 1 cup raw organic honey
- ¼ cup water
- Pinch of sea salt

Directions:

1. Place flaxseeds, lemon juice, strawberries, honey, and water in a slow cooker. Cover the lid. Cook on low for 4 hours.
2. Roughly mash fruits and peppers using a wooden spoon; cook until most of liquid has evaporated, stirring frequently. Turn off heat. Cool completely to room temperature before storing in airtight container with tight fitting lid; use as needed.

Recipe 56 - Thyme-Apricot Jam

Ingredients:

- 10 pieces large fresh thyme sprigs, whole
- ½ piece large lemon, fresh juiced
- 2 lbs. apricots, unpeeled, pitted, diced
- 1 cup raw organic honey
- ¼ cup water

Directions:

1. Except for thyme sprigs, place ingredients in a slow cooker. Cover the lid. Cook on low for 4 hours.
2. Roughly mash fruits using a wooden spoon; add in thyme sprigs. Cook until most liquid has evaporated, stirring frequently. Turn off heat.
3. Fish out and discard thyme. Cool completely to room temperature before storing in airtight container; use as needed.

Recipe 57 - Thyme Berry Jam

Ingredients:

- 10 sprigs large fresh thyme, whole
- 1 cup frozen blueberries, thawed
- 1 cup frozen cranberries, thawed
- 1 cup frozen loganberry, thawed
- 1 cup raw organic honey
- ¼ cup water
- ½ piece, large lemon, fresh juiced, pips removed

Directions:

1. Except for thyme sprigs, place ingredients in a slow cooker. Cover the lid. Cook on low for 4 hours.
2. Using potato masher, mash berries; add in thyme sprigs. Cook until most liquid has evaporated, stirring frequently. Turn off heat.
3. Fish out and discard thyme. Cool completely to room temperature before storing in airtight container; use as needed.

Recipe 58 - Vanilla Berry Jam

Ingredients:

- 1 cup frozen blackberries, thawed
- 1 cup frozen blueberries, thawed
- 1 cup frozen cranberries, thawed
- 1 cup raw organic honey
- ¼ cup water
- 1 piece large   vanilla pod, halved lengthwise, insides scraped
- ½ piece large lemon, fresh juiced, pips removed
- Pinch of sea salt

Directions:

1. Place all ingredients (including vanilla pod and scrapings) in the slow cooker. Cover the lid. Cook on low for 4 hours.
2. Using potato masher, mash berries; cook until most of liquid has evaporated, stirring frequently. Turn off heat. Fish out and discard vanilla pods. Cool to room temperature before storing in airtight container; use as needed.

Recipe 59 - Redux Vanilla Berry Jam

Ingredients:

- 1 cup frozen raspberries, thawed
- 1 cup frozen redcurrants, thawed
- 1 cup raw organic honey
- ¼ cup water
- 1 lb. frozen strawberries, thawed, quartered
- 1 piece large   vanilla pod, halved lengthwise, insides scraped
- ½ piece large lemon, fresh juiced, pips removed
- Pinch of sea salt

Directions:

1. Place all ingredients (including vanilla pod and scrapings) in the slow cooker. Cover the lid. Cook on low for 4 hours.
2. Using potato masher, mash berries; cook until most of liquid has evaporated, stirring frequently. Turn off heat. Fish out and discard vanilla pods. Cool to room temperature before storing in airtight container; use as needed.

Recipe 60 – Holiday Flan

Ingredients:

For the flan

- 3 oz. bittersweet chocolate, broken into chunks
- 1 can coconut milk
- ½ cup coconut sugar
- 2 eggs
- 2 egg yolks

For the caramel

- ¾ cup coconut sugar
- 1/3 cup water
- ¼ cup slivered almonds, toasted

Directions:

1. To make the flan, place chocolate in a saucepan. Add coconut milk and sugar. Stir until the sugar dissolves. Pour over chocolate. Store the mixture well until the chocolate has melted.
2. To make the caramel sauce, bring coconut sugar and water to a boil. Cook for 6 minutes until a syrupy consistency is achieved. Pour in a dish until all sides are well coated.
3. Meanwhile, in a bowl, beat eggs and egg yolks. Add chocolate mixture. Beat constantly until well incorporated. Pour caramel coated dish. Cover with foil. Place dish inside the slow cooker. Add water. Cover the lid. Cook on low for 4 hours. Remove and refrigerate overnight.
4. When ready to serve, remove foil. Serve with caramel sauce.

Recipe 61 – Pears Poached in Green Tea

Ingredients:

- 3 cups boiling water
- 2 tbsp. green tea leaves
- ½ cup liquid honey
- 1 tsp. lemon zest, grated
- 1 gingerroot, grated
- 1 tsp. pure almond extract
- 8 pears, peeled, cord
- ½ cup toasted almonds

Directions:

1. Combine boiling water and green tea leaves in a pot. Allow to steep for 5 minutes. Strain through fine sieve. Transfer into the slow cooker.
2. Add honey, lemon zest, ginger, almond extract, and pears. Cover the lid. Cook on low for 6 hours. Cover and chill overnight. Serve with toasted almonds.

Recipe 62 – Holiday Ginger Cake

Ingredients:

- 3 balls stem ginger, sliced thinly

- 2 tbsp. oil

- ¾ cup maple syrup

- 1 ½ cups sugar

- ½ tsp. baking soda

- 1 ¼ cups wholemeal self-rising flour

- 1 cup applesauce

- 1 ½ tsp. ground ginger

- 1/3 cup almond milk

- 2 tbsp. stem ginger syrup

Directions:

1. Line a loaf tin with greaseproof paper. Arrange stem ginger on to the base of the loaf tin.

2. In a saucepan, pour oil, maple syrup, and sugar. Stir until sugar dissolves. Remove from heat and allow to stand for 15 minutes.

3. Stir in baking soda, flour, applesauce, ginger, and milk into the syrup mixture. Mix until well combined. Pour mixture into the loaf tin.

4. Cover with plastic wrap. Place tin in the slow cooker. Pour boiling water. Cover the lid. Cook on low for 8 hours.

5. Remove tin and let the cake cool. Discard lining paper. Stem ginger syrup over the cake. Serve.

Recipe 63 - Apricot and Nuts Pudding

Ingredients:

- 2 tbsp. extra virgin olive oil

- ½ cup dried apricots, halved

- ½ cup pecan, halved

- 3 tbsp. maple syrup

- 1 cup applesauce

- ¾ cup brown sugar

- 1 orange rind, finely grated

- 1 ½ cup self-rising flour

- 1 orange juice

Directions:

1. Oil a pudding basin. Scatter apricots and pecan nuts into the basin. Drizzle in maple syrup.

2. Meanwhile, combine applesauce and sugar in a bowl. Beat well until a creamy consistency is achieved. Fold in orange rind and flour. Pour orange juice. Mix well. Spoon the mixture into the basin.

3. Oil greaseproof paper. Make a pleat into the center and place side down over the top of the pudding basin. Cover with foil. Cover the lid. Cook on low for 8 hours or on high for 4 hours.

4. Lift pudding out of the slow cooker. Discard paper and foil. Transfer to a serving dish.

Recipe 64 - Yummy Christmas Pudding

Ingredients:

- 1 tbsp. olive oil

- 1 cup almond milk

- 1 cup self-rising flour

- 1 cup raisins

- 1 cup currants

- 1 tsp. baking soda

- 1 ½ cups white breadcrumbs

- 1 ¼ cup brown sugar

- 2 tsp. mixed spice

- ¼ cup applesauce

Directions:

1. Oil a pudding basin. Mix milk, flour, raisins, currants, baking soda, breadcrumbs, brown sugar, applesauce, and mixed spice in a bowl. Spoon into the prepared basin. Cover with foil.

2. Put basin into the slow cooker. Pour enough just enough water. Cover with lid. Cook on low for 8 hours.

3. Lift basin from the slow cooker. Discard foil. Transfer to a serving plate. Serve.

Recipe 65 - Holiday Fruit Bowl Chutney

Ingredients:

- 2 apples, roughly chopped

- 2 peaches, roughly chopped

- 1 lb. tomatoes, roughly chopped

- ¾ cup dried apricots, finely chopped

- ½ cup raisins

- 2 red onions, finely chopped

- 4 garlic cloves, crushed

- 2/3 cup vegan malt vinegar

- 1 star anise

- 2 tsp. wholegrain mustard

- 4 tbsp. dark brown sugar

- Pinch of salt

Directions:

1. Place apples, peaches, tomatoes, apricots, raisins, onions, garlic, malt vinegar, star anise, mustard, sugar, and salt in a slow cooker. Cover the lid. Cook on low for 6 hours.

2. Meanwhile, in a food processor, pour a ladleful of chutney. Process until smooth.

3. Spoon chutney into a jar. Cover and seal tightly with a lid. Store in the fridge.

Recipe 66 - Crème Caramels

Ingredients:

- 2 tbsp. olive oil

- ¾ cup brown sugar

- ½ cup water

- 1 ¼ cup coconut milk

- 1 stem ginger, finely chopped

- 2 tbsp. maple syrup

- 1 cup applesauce

Directions:

1. Oil pudding basin.

2. Meanwhile, pour water and sugar in a saucepan. Bring to a boil. Divide between basins, making sure the base is coated with caramel. Scatter chopped ginger into each pudding basin.

3. Pour coconut milk, stem ginger syrup, and maple syrup into the saucepan. Whisk applesauce into the mixture. Strain back into the saucepan using a sieve.

4. Divide milk mixture between basins. Cover with foil. Put inside the slow cooker. Pour boiling water enough to cover up the sides of the basin.

5. Cover the lid. Cook on low for 5 hours. Remove puddings and dip into hot water for 1 minute. Turn upside down, shake, and serve.

Recipe 67 - Three Fruit Curd

Ingredients:

- 4 tbsp. olive oil

- 2 cups brown sugar

- Lemon grind

- Lemon juice

- Orange rind

- Orange juice

- Lime rind

- Lime juice

- 1 cup applesauce

Directions:

1. Heat oil in a saucepan. Stir in sugar, lemon rind and juice, orange, and lime. Whisk applesauce. Cover basin with foil.

2. Place bowl inside the slow cooker. Pour boiling water just enough to half fill the pudding basin. Cover the lid. Cook on low for 4 hours.

3. Spoon mixture into the jar. Cover and seal tightly with a lid. Store in the fridge.

Recipe 68 – Potato and Broccoli Stew

Ingredients:

- 4 small red potatoes, sliced into thick chunks
- 5 garlic cloves, crushed
- ½ cup broccoli, chopped
- 1 small onion, diced
- 8 oz. jarred fire-roasted tomatoes, not drained
- 3 cups vegetable stock
- 15 oz. canned white cannellini beans, rinsed and drained
- ½ tbsp. dried Italian seasoning
- Pinch of sea salt

Directions:

1. Using your crockpot slow cooker, layer potatoes and garlic. Tip in onion and broccoli on top. Pour tomatoes with juice and vegetable stock. Scatter the beans. Season with Italian seasoning and salt.

2. Secure the lid. Cook on low for 6 hours. Adjust seasoning if needed. Turn off the heat.

3. Serve by ladling equal portion in bowls.

Recipe 69 – Spicy Barbecue Beans

Ingredients:

- ¾ lb. dried white beans, soaked in water for at least 8 hours
- 1 small onion, diced
- 3 garlic cloves, crushed
- ¾ tbsp. molasses
- ¾ tbsp. spicy brown mustard
- ¾ cup barbecue sauce, organic
- ½ tsp. Tabasco sauce
- 2 cups water
- ¾ cup freshly brewed coffee

Directions:

1. Drain soaked beans. Rinse and drain again. Scatter beans into the slow cooker.

2. Tip in onion, garlic, molasses, mustard, barbecue sauce and Tabasco sauce. Mix until well combined.

3. Meanwhile, mix water and freshly brewed coffee. Pour onto the crockpot slow cooker. Stir well. Secure the lid. Cook on low for 6 hours.

4. Once it hit the 6th hour cooking time, uncover the lid. Cook for an additional 30 minutes.

5. Scoop 1 cup of the mixture and transfer to a food processor. Process until smooth. Put back into the slow cooker. Stir well until the sauce thickens. Serve.

Recipe 70 - Slow-Cooked Tilapia Fillets

Ingredients:

- 1 ½ tsp can sugar
- 4 ½ tbsp. warm water
- 1 ½ lb. thick, boneless tilapia fillets
- 3 garlic cloves, crushed
- 2 large onion, chopped
- 4 ½ tbsp. lime juice, freshly squeezed
- Pinch of sea salt
- Pinch of freshly ground black pepper

Directions:

1. In a small mixing bowl, put together sugar and warm water. Mix. Add in tilapia fillets. Make sure to coat well. Layer the fish in the crockpot slow cooker.

2. Put garlic and onion all over the fish. Add some lime juice. Season with salt and pepper.

3. Secure the lid. Cook on low for 6 hours. Serve.

Recipe 71 - King Prawn Curry

Ingredients:

- 2 lbs. raw king prawns, peeled and deveined
- 2 small onions, chopped
- 5 garlic cloves, crushed
- 12 oz. halved cherry tomatoes
- 1 ½ cups sieved tomatoes
- 12 oz. frozen peas
- 1 ½ tsp. sunflower oil
- Pinch of sea salt
- Pinch of freshly ground black pepper
- 3 tbsp. chopped fresh cilantro

Directions:

1. Layer prawns inside the crockpot slow cooker. Spread garlic, onion, cherry tomatoes, sieved tomatoes, and peas all over the prawns. Pour sunflower oil.

2. Secure the lid. Cook on high for 4 hours. Transfer to a serving dish. Sprinkle cilantro. Serve.

Recipe 72 - Chickpea Soup with Veggies

Ingredients:

- 2 cups beef bone broth

- ½ cup canned chickpeas, rinsed, drained

- 1 piece large garlic clove, minced

- 1 piece small onion, minced

- 1 can, 15 oz., diced and peeled tomatoes

- ½ cup frozen green peas, thawed

- 1 piece small sweet potato, peeled, minced

- 1 piece large fresh bay leaf

- 1 piece large celery ribs and leaves, minced

- 1 piece medium carrot, tops removed, diced

- ⅛ tsp. dried rosemary, roughly torn

- ⅛ tsp. sea salt

- ⅛ tsp. black pepper

- ⅛ cup, loosely packed fresh basil leaves, minced

- 1 piece small zucchini, unpeeled, diced

- ½ piece, small cabbage head, julienned

- ⅛ cup freshly shredded Parmesan cheese

- ¼ tsp. fresh cilantro, minced

Directions:

1. Pour beef bone broth into the crockpot slow cooker. Add in chickpeas, garlic clove, onion, tomatoes, green peas, sweet potato, bay leaf, celery ribs, carrot, and rosemary. Season with salt and pepper.
2. Secure the lid. Cook on low for 6 hours. 1 hour before the cooking time, toss in basil leaves, zucchini, and small cabbage. Secure the lid. Cook for an additional 1 hour.
3. Serve by ladling into bowls. Garnish with Parmesan cheese and cilantro.

Recipe 73 - Ginger Grouper Soup

Ingredients:

- 1 tsp. coconut oil

- 2 cups fish bone broth

- 1 cup water

- 2 pieces grouper fillet, trimmed well

- 1 piece large red onion, minced

- 1 piece large garlic clove, grated

- 1 piece thumb-sized ginger, peeled, crushed with flat-side of knife

- 1 piece potato, peeled, cubed

- ½ tsp. fish sauce, add more if desired

- Pinch of sea salt

- Pinch of black pepper, to taste

- 1 piece small cabbage, cored, quartered

Directions:

1. In a nonstick skillet, heat the coconut oil. Once the oil is hot, sauté garlic, onion, and ginger for 2 minutes.
2. Transfer contents of skillet into the crockpot slow cooker. Pour bone broth, water, groper fillet, red onion, garlic, ginger, potato, and fish sauce. Season with salt and pepper.
3. Secure the lid. Cook on high for 4 hours.
4. Before the end of cooking time, stir in the cabbage. Secure the lid. Cook for another 30 minutes on high. Turn off the heat. Transfer into a serving dish.

5. Serve by ladling stew into bowls.

Recipe 74 - Cod Tagine

Ingredients:

- 1 ½ tbsp. paprika
- 1 ½ tsp. ground ginger
- 1 ½ tbsp. ground cumin
- 1 cup olive oil
- 1/3 cup dry white wine
- 3 tbsp. fresh cilantro, chopped
- 1/3 cup lemon juice, freshly squeezed
- Pinch of sea salt
- 2 ¼ lb. cod, washed, sliced into equal portions
- 3 large onions, diced
- 5 garlic cloves, minced
- 2/3 cup seafood or vegetable stock
- ¾ cup sliced pimiento-stuffed green olives
- 3 bay leaves
- Cayenne pepper
- Freshly ground black pepper

Directions:

1. In a small mixing bowl, put together ground ginger, paprika, and cumin. Set aside.

2. In another bowl, combine oil, wine, spice mix, cilantro, lemon juice, salt, and cayenne. In a resealable freezer bag, mix ¾ cup of oil with the lemon juice, wine, cilantro, spice mix, and a pinch of salt and cayenne. Transfer contents in a zip lock bag. Place the cod fillets inside. Marinate and put inside the freezer for 2 hours.

3. Once ready, pour contents of the zip lock bag including the marinade into the slow cooker. Layer onion and garlic.

4. Secure the lid. Cook on low for 6 hours. Turn off the heat. Discard bay leaves. Transfer to a platter. Serve.

Recipe 75 - Squash and Apple Soup

Ingredients:

- ¼ tsp. olive oil

- 1 piece large shallot, minced

- 1 piece large garlic clove, grated

- Water

- 2 cups beef bone broth

- ½ cup canned, diced and peeled tomatoes

- 1 piece large butternut squash, peeled, cubed

- 1 piece large leek, chopped

- 1 piece small apple, cored, chopped

- Pinch of sea salt

- Pinch of black pepper, to taste

- 1 dollop chilled sour cream, divided

- ¼ tsp. fresh parsley leaves and tender stems, minced

Directions:

1. Pour oil into a nonstick skillet set over medium heat. Sauté shallot and garlic for 2 minutes.

2. Pour just enough water and bone broth. Tip in tomatoes, squash, leek, and apple. Season with salt and pepper.

3. Secure the lid of the crockpot slow cooker. Cook on high for 4 hours. Turn off the heat. Allow the mixture to cool before processing in a food processor. Blend until smooth.

4. Serve by ladling equal amount into bowls. Garnish with chilled sour cream and sprinkle with parsley. Serve.

Recipe 76 - Tuna in Brine Casserole

Ingredients:

- 12 oz. canned tuna packed in brine, drained thoroughly
- 3 cups frozen peas
- 12 oz. fresh button mushrooms, sliced thinly
- 3 tbsp. organic butter or ghee
- 1/3 cup rice flour
- 1 ½ cups vegetable or chicken stock
- 1 ½ cups low fat or nut-based milk
- ¾ cup freshly grated Parmesan cheese
- ¾ tsp sea salt
- ¾ tsp freshly ground black pepper

Directions:

1. Pour tuna in brine into the crockpot slow cooker. Scatter peas and mushrooms.

2. Meanwhile, heat the butter in a saucepan. Once hot and melted, stir in flour. Pour vegetable broth and milk. Mix well. Add in cheese.

3. Once the mixture is hot, pour onto the slow cooker. Season with salt and pepper. Mix well. Secure the lid. Cook on low for 8 hours or on high for 4 hours.

4. Serve with pasta or over a bed of hot rice.

Recipe 77 - Lemon Mustard Haddock

Ingredients:

- 2 tbsp. Dijon mustard
- 5 tbsp. freshly squeezed lemon juice
- 1 ½ tsp. paprika
- 9 haddock fillets
- ¾ cup shredded low fat or vegan mozzarella cheese

Directions:

1. This recipe requires the use of an aluminum foil.

2. In a small mixing bowl, put together, mustard, lemon juice, and paprika. Mix well. Set aside.

3. Prepare the aluminum foil. Put each fillet at the center of each sheet. Spoon the mustard lemon mixture all over the fillet. Top with mozzarella cheese.

4. Seal the foil. Make sure to create tight packets. Crimp edges. Layer fish into the crockpot slow cooker. Secure the lid. Cook on high for 4 hours. Serve.

Recipe 78 - Tuna Rice Porridge

Ingredients:

- ½ tsp. olive oil

- 1 piece small onion, minced

- 1 piece small garlic, minced

- 3 cups fish bone broth

- ¼ cup frozen green peas, thawed

- ¼ cup sticky rice, rinsed, drained

- 1 can, 5 oz. tuna chunks in brine, do not drain

- ⅛ tsp. fish sauce

- Pinch of sea salt

- Pinch white pepper, to taste

- ¼ cup fresh chives, minced

- 1 tsp. lime juice, freshly squeezed

Directions:

1. Pour olive oil into a medium-sized saucepan. Sauté onion and garlic for 2 minutes. Transfer contents into the crockpot slow cooker.

2. Pour fish bone broth, green peas, rice, tuna chunks in brine, and fish sauce. Season with salt and pepper.

3. Secure the lid. Cook on low for 6 hours. Adjust taste if needed. Turn off heat. Serve by ladling porridge into individual bowls. Garnish with chives. Squeeze lime juice. Serve.

Recipe 79 - Seafood Stew

Ingredients:

- ¼ cup olive oil

- 2 pieces, large garlic clove, minced

- 1 tsp. dried pepper flakes

- 1 piece large fresh bay leaf

- 3 cups fish bone broth

- ½ cup fresh basil leaves, roughly torn

- 2½ pounds clams, shells scrubbed clean

- 1½ pounds green mussels, shells scrubbed clean

- 1 lb. prawns, peeled, deveined, halved lengthwise

- 1 can, 15 oz. diced and peeled tomatoes

- ⅛ tsp. fish sauce

- ½ tsp. white sugar

- Pinch of sea salt, to taste

- ⅛ cup fresh parsley, minced, for garnish, optional

Directions:

1. Pour oil into the crockpot slow cooker. Cook garlic, pepper flakes, and bay leaf for 1 minute.
2. Pour fish bone broth, basil leaves, clams, mussels, and prawns. Tip in tomatoes. Season with fish sauce, sugar, and salt.
3. Secure the lid. Cook on high for 4 hours.
4. Discard shells that did not open. Turn off heat.
5. Serve by ladling equal portions into bowls. Garnish with parsley.

Recipe 80 - Butter Bean and Veggies Stew

Ingredients:

- 1 large onion, sliced into thick rings
- 3 garlic cloves, crushed
- 34 oz. sweet potatoes, peeled and sliced thinly
- 2 celery ribs, chopped
- 1 ½ lb. cauliflower florets, chopped
- ¾ tsp. ground cinnamon
- 3 tbsp. pureed tomato
- 12 oz. canned butter beans, rinsed and drained
- 3 oz. sultanas
- 3 oz. chopped almonds
- 21 oz. chopped tomatoes
- 1 ½ cups vegetable stock, low sodium
- Sea salt
- Freshly ground black pepper

Directions:

1. Layer sweet potatoes into the crockpot slow cook cooker. Add butter beans, almonds, tomatoes, cauliflower, garlic, onion, almonds, sultanas, celery, pureed tomato, and chopped tomatoes. Pour vegetable stock. Season with salt and pepper. Put a dash of cinnamon.

2. Secure the lid. Cook on low for 8 hours. Transfer to a serving bowl. Serve.

Recipe 81 - Pork Broth in Lemongrass

Ingredients:

- 2 tbsp. coconut vinegar

- 2 ½ pounds raw pork bones, include bone-in/skin-on cuts

- 2 pieces large shallots, peeled, quartered

- 1 piece thumb-sized ginger, crushed

- 2 pieces large lemongrass bulbs, crushed

- 1 piece large sweet potato, coarsely chopped

- 2 pieces large whole dried bay leaves

- 1 tsp. heaping black peppercorns

- Pinch of coarse-grained sea salt, to taste

- Water

Directions:

1. Except for water, pour vinegar and add pork bones, shallots, ginger, lemongrass bulbs, sweet potato, bay leaves, black peppercorns, and salt in a crock pot slow cooker set over medium heat. Pour just enough water to submerge ingredients. Stir once.

2. Secure the lid. Set the slow cooker at medium heat. Cook on low for 8 hours or on high for 4 hours.

3. Turn off machine. Cool broth completely to room temperature. Adjust seasoning if needed. Discard solids. Use a fine-meshed sieve draped over a colander.

4. Pour broth in a freezer-safe container. Freeze for 2 hours or until ready to use.

5. To reheat, scoop up desired amount of broth into a cup or bowl. Reheat in the microwave oven. Serve.

Recipe 82 - Unsalted Fish Broth

Ingredients:

- 4 lbs. fish heads and frames, combination of raw and cooked fish

- Olive oil for drizzling

For broth

- 6 cups water

- 2 tbsp. apple cider vinegar

- 2 pieces large carrots, roughly chopped

- 2 pieces large celery ribs, coarsely chopped

- 1 piece large onion, quartered

- 1 piece thumb-sized ginger

- 1 tsp. whole black peppercorns

Directions:

1. Preheat the oven to 350°F. Line a roasting tin with aluminum foil.

2. Layer fish heads and frames in a roasting tin. Drizzle in olive oil. Roast for 20 minutes or until almost crisp and fragrant. Remove tin from oven.

3. Transfer contents into a crockpot slow cooker.

4. Secure the lid. Set the slow cooker at medium heat. Cook on low for 8 hours or on high for 4 hours.

5. Turn off machine. Cool broth completely to room temperature. Adjust seasoning if needed. Discard solids. Use a fine-meshed sieve draped over a colander.

6. Pour broth in a freezer-safe container. Freeze for 2 hours or until ready to use.

7. To reheat, scoop up desired amount of broth into a cup or bowl. Reheat in the microwave oven. Serve.

Recipe 83 - Unsalted Vegetable Stock

- 2 tbsp. olive oil

Flavor base

- 2 pieces large shallot, diced

- 2 pieces large carrots, sliced into inch-thick disks

- 2 pieces large leeks, chopped

- 2 pieces large celery stalks, chopped

For the broth

- 8 cups water

- 2 pieces large fresh whole bay leaves

- 1 piece large garlic head, cloves peeled

- 1 generous pinch fresh oregano

- 1 generous pinch fresh parsley

- 1 generous pinch fresh thyme

Vegetable scraps/leftovers, roughly chopped

- Bell pepper tops and trimmings
- Asparagus stems
- Kale stems
- Mushrooms stems and trimmings
- Herbs and spices

Directions:

1. Pour oil into a non-stick skillet. Add shallots, carrots, leeks, and celery stalks. Sauté for 5 to 7 minutes.
2. Transfer contents into the crockpot slow cooker. Pour broth ingredients and vegetable scraps into the crockpot.

3. Secure the lid. Set the slow cooker at medium heat. Cook on low for 8 hours or on high for 4 hours.

4. Turn off machine. Cool broth completely to room temperature. Adjust seasoning if needed. Discard solids. Use a fine-meshed sieve draped over a colander.

5. Pour broth in a freezer-safe container. Freeze for 2 hours or until ready to use.

6. To reheat, scoop up desired amount of broth into a cup or bowl. Reheat in the microwave oven. Serve.

Recipe 84 - Beef and Vegetable Broth

Ingredients:

- 2½ lbs. beef bones, preferably with marrow

For broth

- 3 tbsp. balsamic vinegar
- 1 tsp. dried oregano
- 2 pieces large celery ribs, coarsely chopped
- 1 tbsp. dried rosemary
- 2 pieces large whole dried bay leaves
- 1 tsp. black peppercorns, lightly cracked
- Pinch of coarse-grained sea salt, to taste
- Water

Roasting vegetables

- 3 pieces small garlic heads, tops sliced off exposing cloves
- 2 pieces large shallots, halved
- 1 piece large sweet potato, coarsely chopped
- 1 pieces large carrot, top roughly chopped
- ¼ piece small butternut squash, cubed
- 1 piece small red bell pepper, cubed

- Olive oil for drizzling

Directions:

1. Preheat the oven to 350°F. Line a roasting tin with aluminum foil.
2. Layer beef bones in roasting tin, marrow side up. Roast beef bones for 25 minutes or until browned all over. Flip and roast for another 10 minutes. Remove from the oven.
3. Place roasting vegetables into the baking sheet except for garlic cloves. Mix well. Place garlic heads in the corners of the baking sheet. Season with salt. Drizzle in olive oil. Roast vegetables for 20 minutes.
4. For the broth, transfer everything into the crockpot slow cooker. Except for water, pour in remaining broth ingredients. Stir once.
5. Secure the lid. Set the slow cooker at medium heat. Cook on low for 8 hours or on high for 4 hours.

6. Turn off machine. Cool broth completely to room temperature. Adjust seasoning if needed. Discard solids. Use a fine-meshed sieve draped over a colander.

7. Pour broth in a freezer-safe container. Freeze for 2 hours or until ready to use.

8. To reheat, scoop up desired amount of broth into a cup or bowl. Reheat in the microwave oven. Serve.

Recipe 85 - Roasted Vegetable Stock

Ingredients:

Flavor base

- 1 piece large garlic head, cloves separated, crushed

- 1 piece large shallot, chopped

- ½ lb. fresh portabella mushrooms, halved

- 1 piece large carrot, unpeeled, cubed

- 1 piece large red bell pepper, cubed

- 1 piece small acorn squash, cubed

- Olive oil for drizzling

- Pinch of sea salt

- Pinch of black pepper, to taste

For the broth

- 6 cups water

- ½ cup apple cider vinegar

- ½ cup canned crushed tomatoes

- 1 piece large fresh whole bay leaf

- 1 generous pinch fresh parsley, torn

- 1 generous pinch fresh thyme, torn

- 1 tbsp. freshly-cracked black peppercorns

Directions:

1. Preheat the oven to 425°F. Line a roasting tin with aluminum foil.

2. Put garlic, shallot, portabella mushrooms, carrot, red bell pepper, and squash in the crockpot slow cooker. Toss well to combine. Drizzle olive oil on top. Season lightly with salt and pepper.

3. Secure the lid. Set the slow cooker at medium heat. Cook on low for 8 hours or on high for 4 hours.

4. Before the last hour, pour in apple cider vinegar and deglaze. Turn off heat when vinegar starts to bubble.

5. Pour deglazing liquid. Tip in tomatoes, bay leaf, parsley, thyme, and black peppercorns.

6. Secure the lid. Set the slow cooker at medium heat. Cook on high for 2 hours.

7. Turn off machine. Cool broth completely to room temperature. Adjust seasoning if needed. Discard solids. Use a fine-meshed sieve draped over a colander.

8. Pour broth in a freezer-safe container. Freeze for 2 hours or until ready to use.

9. To reheat, scoop up desired amount of broth into a cup or bowl. Reheat in the microwave oven. Serve.

Recipe 86 – Healthy Chicken Soup

Ingredients:

For the Soup

- 1 piece small onion, minced

- ¼ lb. chicken thigh fillets, minced

- ½ tsp. chili powder

- ½ tsp. black pepper

- 4 cups chicken broth

- 1 can, 15 oz. diced tomatoes

- 1 piece small fresh jalapeño pepper, minced

- 1 tbsp. olive oil

- 1 tsp. cumin powder

- 1 tsp. sea salt

Garnishes, optional

- 1 piece large lime, sliced into wedges

- ½ just ripe avocado, sliced into ¼-inch-thick half moons

- Generous pinch fresh cilantro, minced

Directions:

1. Pour oil into a large saucepan set over medium heat. Cook onions, chicken, cumin, jalapeño, chili powder, black pepper, and sea salt. Cook for 10 minutes or until onions are limp and chicken is cooked through. Stir often.
2. Except for garnishes, pour in remaining ingredients. Stir well to combine.
3. Secure the lid. Set the slow cooker at medium heat. Cook on low for 8 hours or on high for 4 hours.
4. Turn down heat. Let warm for 10 minutes. Remove from heat. Cool slightly. Ladle equal amount of soup into individual bowls.
5. Garnish each bowl lime, avocado, and cilantro. Serve.

Recipe 87 - Spicy Shrimp and Coconut Soup

Ingredients:

Garnishes

- 1 piece large lime, sliced into wedges

- ⅛ cup fresh cilantro, minced

For the soup

- 1 can, 15 oz. straw mushrooms, halved lengthwise

- 2 tbsp. fish sauce

- 1 piece large lime, freshly juiced

- 1 can, 15 oz. coconut cream

For the Soup base

- 4 cups shrimp broth

- 4 garlic cloves, peeled, crushed

- 1 piece large onion, peeled, quartered

- 1 piece thumb-sized ginger, peeled, crushed

- 2 pieces large tomatoes, quartered

- 2 pieces large lemongrass bulbs

- 2 pieces large fresh kaffir lime leaves

- 2 pieces large banana chili

- 1½ lb. large shrimps, peeled, deveined

Directions:

1. For the soup base: Pour shrimp broth. Garlic cloves, onion, ginger, tomatoes, lemongrass bulbs, kaffir leaves, banana chili, and prawns in a crockpot slow cooker.
2. Secure the lid. Set the slow cooker at medium heat. Cook on high for 4 hours.
3. Allow to warm through for 15 minutes. Turn off heat. Cool to room temperature. Discard solids.
4. Pour broth in a freezer-safe container. Freeze for 2 hours or until ready to use. To reheat, scoop up desired amount of broth into a cup or bowl. Reheat in the microwave oven. Serve.
5. For the soup, pour 2 cups soup base/broth in a crockpot slow cooker.
6. Secure the lid. Set the slow cooker at medium heat. Cook on high for 2 hours.
7. Before the last hour, stir coconut cream and lime juice. Adjust seasoning if needed.
8. Garnish with cilantro. Ladle desired amount into bowl. Squeeze lime juice over dish. Serve.

Recipe 88 – Spicy Mushroom and Vegetables Soup

Ingredients:

- 2 tbsp. olive oil

- 1 piece large garlic clove, minced

- 1 piece large onion, minced

- 1 piece large red bell pepper, deseeded, diced

- 1 piece large chili, deseeded, diced

- 1 piece large jalapeño pepper, deseeded, diced

- 2½ cups vegetable stock

- 1 piece small yellow summer squash, deseeded, cubed

- 1 piece small acorn squash, deseeded, cubed

- ½ tsp. coriander powder

- ¼ tsp. sea salt

- ¼ tsp. black pepper

- 1 piece small zucchini, cubed

- 1 can, 15 oz. whole button mushrooms, halved

- 1 can, 15 oz. straw mushrooms, halved

Directions:

1. Pour oil into a saucepan set oven set over medium heat. Sauté garlic and onions for 3 minutes or until fragrant and translucent.
2. Stir in red bell pepper, chili, and jalapeño. Cook for 10 minutes. Transfer contents of the saucepan into the crockpot slow cooker.
3. Pour vegetable stock, yellow squash, and acorn. Season with coriander, salt, and pepper.

4. Secure the lid. Set the slow cooker at medium heat. Cook on high for 4 hours. Allow soup to warm for 15 minutes. Stir in zucchini and mushrooms. Cook on high for another 1 hour.

5. Taste. Adjust seasoning if needed. Ladle equal amount of soup in bowls. Serve.

Recipe 89 - Chunky Cauliflower Soup

Ingredients:

- 2 cups vegetable stock

- 1 piece small sweet potato, diced

- 1 piece large carrot, diced

- 2 cups cauliflowers, sliced into bite-sized florets

- 1 cup yellow summer squash, deseeded, diced

- 2 cups, fresh spinach, roughly chopped

- ¼ cup almond cheese

- 1 tsp. sea salt

- Pinch of black pepper, to taste

- 1 tbsp. fresh parsley, minced, for garnish

Directions:

1. Pour vegetable stock and add in sweet potato, carrots, cauliflower florets, and squash into the crockpot slow cooker.
2. Secure the lid. Set the slow cooker at medium heat. Cook on high for 4 hours.
3. Before the final hour, add in spinach leaves. Cover the lid and cook on high for another 30 minutes.
4. Taste. Adjust seasoning if needed. Sprinkle almond cheese. Season with salt and pepper. Allow to warm for 10 minutes.
5. Ladle into soup bowls. Garnish with parsley. Serve.

Recipe 90 – Fish and Shellfish Soup

Ingredients:

- 2 tbsp. olive oil

- 2 pieces large garlic cloves, minced

- 1 piece large onion, minced

- 2 pieces large celery stalks, strings removed, minced

- 1 piece medium fennel bulb, julienned

- 2 pieces large fresh bay leaves, whole

- ½ tsp. red pepper flakes

- 1 tsp. dried oregano

- 3 cups fish broth

- 1 can crushed tomatoes

- ½ tbsp. tomato paste

- ½ lb. frozen large shrimps or prawns, thawed

- ½ lb. frozen halibut fish fillets thawed, sliced into large cubes

- ½ lb. frozen squid rings, thawed

- 1 lb. mussels, shells scrubbed clean

- 1 lb. fresh little neck clams, soaked in salted water for 1 hour before cooking

- 1 can (whole) clams in natural clam juice, separate clams from juice

- Pinch of sea salt

- Pinch of black pepper, to taste

- 1 generous pinch fresh parsley, minced

Directions:
1. Pour oil into a saucepan set over medium heat.
2. Stir-fry garlic and onions for 3 minutes or until aromatic and translucent. Tip in celery, fennel bulb, bay leaves, red pepper flakes, and oregano. Stir constantly to prevent from burning and crusting.
3. Pour liquids. Season with salt and pepper.
4. Secure the lid. Set the slow cooker at medium heat. Cook on high for 4 hours.
5. Pour fish broth, tomatoes, and tomato paste. Add in shrimp, fish fillets, and squid rings. Secure the lid and cook on high for another 2 hours.
6. Before the final hour, first, secure lid. Let soup simmer for 5 minutes. Add in mussels, neck clams, and clam meat. Season with salt and pepper. Secure the lid and cook for another hour on high.
7. Discard any unopened shellfish, and bay leaves. Allow to cool before ladling into soup bowls.
8. Garnish with fresh parsley. Serve.

Recipe 91 - Buffalo Wings Stew

Ingredients:

- 2 lbs. boneless, skinless chicken breasts, diced
- 1 large white onion, diced
- 1 cup baby carrots, chopped
- 9 garlic cloves, minced
- 1 ½ cups chopped celery
- 5 red potatoes, cubed
- 9 cups chicken stock
- 1 ¼ cups prepared buffalo wing sauce
- 1.5 oz. packet ranch salad dressing mix
- 3 cups shredded mozzarella cheese
- ¾ cup crumbled blue cheese

Directions:

1. Layer chicken breasts into the crockpot slow cooker. Sprinkle onion, carrots, garlic, celery, and red potato. Pour salad dressing on top

2. Meanwhile, in a mixing bowl, combine buffalo wing sauce and broth. Combine the broth and buffalo wing sauce until well incorporated, then pour over the dressing mix.

3. Secure the lid. Set the slow cooker at medium heat. Cook on low for 8 hours.

4. Before the end of cooking time, sprinkle mozzarella and blue cheese. Serve.

Recipe 92 – Easy Turkey Stew

Ingredients:

- 3 ¼ lbs. skinless turkey drumsticks
- 1 large onion, diced
- 6 oz. jalapeno peppers, chopped
- 1 can, 21 oz. chopped tomatoes
- 1 can, 21 oz. corn kernels
- 5 cups low sodium chicken stock
- 1 ½ tsp. chili powder
- 1 ½ tbsp. ground cumin
- ¾ tsp. sea salt

Directions:

1. Lay turkey drumsticks into the crockpot slow cooker. Sprinkle onion, jalapeños, tomatoes, and corn.

5. Pour chicken stock. Add chili powder, cumin, and salt. Secure the lid. Set the slow cooker at medium heat. Cook on low for 8 hours.
6. Before serving, shred turkey bones. Return to the crockpot and stir well. Serve.

Recipe 93 - Mustard Chicken and Veggies

Ingredients:

- 1 ½ lbs. skinless chicken breasts, rinsed, pat-dry
- 1 ½ tbsp. whole wheat flour
- 2 cups chicken stock, low sodium
- 3 leeks, chopped
- 1 cup spinach
- 3 tbsp. Dijon mustard
- 1 ½ tsp. mustard powder
- 1 ½ bay leaves
- Sea salt
- Freshly ground black pepper

Directions:

1. Dredge chicken breast in the flour. Set aside.

2. Heat the skillet set over medium flame. Cook chicken breasts for 5 minutes or until browned all over. Transfer contents of the skillet into the slow cooker.

3. Add chicken stock, leeks, spinach, Dijon mustard, mustard powder, bay leaves, salt, and pepper.

4. Secure the lid. Set the slow cooker at medium heat. Cook on low for 8 hours.

5. Before serving, chop chicken into strips. Transfer to a serving bowl. Pour sauce and veggies on top. Serve.

Recipe 94 - Chicken Soup with Quail Eggs

Ingredients:

- 3 cups chicken bone broth

- 8 pieces quail eggs, hard-boiled

- ¼ piece, small red bell pepper, sliced diagonally

- 1 piece large napa cabbage leaf, sliced diagonally

- 1 piece small celery rib, sliced diagonally

- ⅛ tsp. rosemary powder

- ⅛ tsp. garlic powder

- ¼ tsp. Spanish paprika powder

- ¼ tsp. fish sauce

- ⅛ tsp. white pepper

- Pinch of sea salt, to taste

- 1 piece large leek, sliced diagonally

Directions:

1. Pour chicken broth, quail eggs, red bell pepper, napa cabbage leaf, celery rib, rosemary powder, garlic powder, paprika powder, fish sauce, salt, and pepper into the crockpot slow cooker.

2. Secure the lid. Set the slow cooker at medium heat. Cook on low for 8 hours.

3. Ladle equal portions into soup bowls. Garnish with leeks. Serve.

Recipe 95 - Chicken Soup with Eggs

Ingredients:

- 3 cups chicken bone broth

- ¼ tsp. fish sauce

- ¼ cup frozen green peas, thawed

- ⅛ tsp. garlic powder

- ⅛ tsp. ginger powder

- ¼ tsp. Spanish paprika powder

- ⅛ tsp. white pepper

- Pinch of sea salt, to taste

- 2 eggs, whisked

- 1 piece bird's eye chili, minced

- 1 piece large leek, sliced diagonally

Directions:

1. Pour chicken broth, fish sauce, green peas, garlic powder, ginger powder, paprika powder, white pepper, and salt in the crockpot slow cooker.

2. Secure the lid. Set the slow cooker at medium heat. Cover the lid and cook on low for 8 hours.

3. Turn off heat immediately. Adjust seasoning, if needed.

4. Ladle equal portions in soup bowls. Garnish with chili and leek. Serve.

Recipe 96 - Italian Chicken Stew

Ingredients:

- 7 lbs. chopped skinless chicken pieces
- Sea salt
- Freshly ground black pepper
- 1 large onion, chopped
- 3 garlic cloves, crushed
- ½ cup pitted green olives
- 2 small red bell peppers, chopped
- 42 oz. chopped tomatoes
- 1 ½ tsp. anchovy paste
- 5 bay leaves
- ½ tsp. dried rosemary
- 3 cups chicken stock

Directions:

1. Season chicken with salt and pepper. Spread the flour on a platter and dredge the chicken in it.

2. Prepare the skillet. Heat the oil. Once hot, cook the chicken for 5 minutes or until browned all over. Transfer cooked chicken into the crockpot slow cooker.

3. Tip in onion, garlic, olives, bell peppers, tomatoes, anchovy paste, bay leaves, and rosemary. Pour stock. Mix well.

4. Secure the lid. Set the slow cooker at medium heat. Cover the lid and cook on low for 8 hours. Serve.

Conclusion

I hope this book has helped you with your holiday cooking dilemma and to be able to gain loads of Christmas recipes that you can prepare using the ever-reliable slow cooker. Now, with your slow cooker as your helpmate, cooking will be twice as fun. With the slow cooker, you can leave it in the kitchen and do other chores and errands during the holiday rush.

The next step is to get to know more about your slow cooker and try out the dishes found in this cookbook. All of the above-mentioned recipes are easy to prepare and follow. Share the cooking tips and recipes you found here with your family and friends. You can also have this cookbook serve as a Christmas gift to your friends and family struggling to find the perfect kitchen appliance to serve as their buddy in the kitchen. After reading this book, you surely will never look at slow cookers the same way again. They are indeed heaven-sent.

Finally, if you enjoyed this book, then I'd like to ask you for a favor, would you be kind enough to leave a review for this book on Amazon? It'd be greatly appreciated!

65039969R00073